Graphing Calculator and Computer Graphing Laboratory Manual Supplement

DEMANA   WAITS   CLEMENS

Graphing Calculator and Computer Graphing Laboratory Manual Supplement

DEMANA   WAITS   CLEMENS

Precalculus Series
Second Edition

ADDISON-WESLEY PUBLISHING COMPANY
Reading, Massachusetts ◆ Menlo Park, California ◆ New York ◆ Don Mills, Ontario
Wokingham, England ◆ Amsterdam ◆ Bonn ◆ Sydney ◆ Singapore ◆ Tokyo ◆ Madrid
San Juan ◆ Milan ◆ Paris

ISBN 0-201-58849-8

1 2 3 4 5 6 7 8 9 10-CRW-96959493

CONTRIBUTORS

Gregory D. Foley
Sam Houston State University

G.T. Springer
Alamo Heights High School–San Antonio, TX

David Lawrence
Southwestern Oklahoma State University

CONTENTS

Graphing Calculator and Computer Graphing Laboratory Manual Supplement

DEMANA   WAITS   CLEMENS

CHAPTER 1

The Casio fx-6300G Graphing Calculator

This brief chapter is intended to acquaint you with the features of the Casio fx-6300G graphing calculator. Its keyboard and operation are almost identical to the fx-7000G, and in most cases, you can follow the instructions given in Chapter 5 of the *Graphing Calculator and Computer Graphing Laboratory Manual*. You are urged to read that chapter after you read this one. This chapter focuses on the differences between the two calculators.

1.1   The Keyboard and Screen

The fx-6300G has no on/off switch. To turn it on, press $\boxed{\text{AC}}$; to turn it off, use the shift function of $\boxed{\text{AC}}$; that is, press $\boxed{\text{SHIFT}}$ $\boxed{\text{OFF}}$.

The keyboard is the same as that of the fx-7000G except that $\boxed{\text{Graph}}$ and $\boxed{\text{Range}}$ have both moved one position to the left and $\boxed{\text{M Disp}}$ and $\boxed{\text{(-)}}$ have been replaced by $\boxed{\text{Trace}}$ and $\boxed{\text{a}^{b}\text{/c}}$, respectively. So on the fx-6300G, the TRACE feature can be accessed directly, and rational-number (fraction) arithmetic is built in.

The most obvious difference between the fx-7000G and the fx-6300G is the screen. The fx-6300G screen is less than half the size of the fx-7000G screen. Press $\boxed{\text{AC}}$ to turn on your calculator. Figure 1.1 shows how the display screen might look. If your screen does not look like this,

- press $\boxed{\text{MODE}}$ $\boxed{+}$ to ensure your calculator is in Computation mode;
- press $\boxed{\text{MODE}}$ **4** $\boxed{\text{EXE}}$ to ensure it is in Degree mode; and
- press $\boxed{\text{MODE}}$ **9** $\boxed{\text{EXE}}$ to ensure it is in Normal display mode.

Your screen should now look like Fig. 1.1.

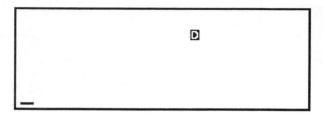

Figure 1.1   The screen as it may appear when you turn
on the fx-6300G.

The outlined 'D' on the screen is called a **display indicator**. In this case, it indicates that the calculator is currently in Degree mode. Various other display indicators are used to indicate mode status, the exponent for scientific notation, or which coordinate (x or y) is being shown when the TRACE feature is active. You will need to press MODE **5** EXE to put your calculator in Radian mode to work through the examples in Chapter 5 of the *Graphing Calculator and Computer Graphing Laboratory Manual*. The upper right-hand portion of the screen is dedicated to display indicators.

The left half of the screen displays graphics in a 39-by-23 pixel window (compared to 95-by-63 on the fx-7000G). Calculations are displayed at the bottom of the screen on a 12-character line. Entries with 12 or more characters scroll off the screen.

1.2 _____ Rational-Number Arithmetic

A useful key available on the fx-6300G is a^b/c . This key is used to enter fractions or mixed numbers. SHIFT d/c converts a mixed number to an improper fraction.

Example 1

Problem Evaluate $\frac{3}{4} + \frac{1}{3}$ and display the rational-number result as a mixed number, in decimal form, and as an improper fraction.

Solution Press

$$3 \quad \boxed{a^b/c} \quad 4 \quad \boxed{+} \quad 1 \quad \boxed{a^b/c} \quad 3$$

to create the command line shown in Fig. 1.2. Notice that the symbol ⌐ is used instead of a slash (/) to separate the numerator from the denominator in each fraction.

Figure 1.2

Press $\boxed{\text{EXE}}$, to display the result as a mixed number (see Fig. 1.3). The **⌟** separates the three parts of the mixed number in the following order: integer part, numerator, denominator. So **1⌟ 1⌟ 12** represents the mixed number $1\frac{1}{12}$.

Figure 1.3

Press $\boxed{a^b/c}$ to convert the result to a decimal (see Fig. 1.4). If you want, press $\boxed{a^b/c}$ again to convert the result back to an improper fraction.

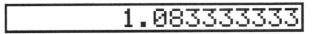

Figure 1.4

Press $\boxed{\text{SHIFT}}$ $\boxed{d/c}$ to convert the result to an improper fraction (see Fig. 1.5).

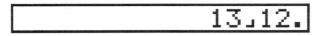

Figure 1.5   Converting to an improper fraction

1.3 ———— Scrolling the Graphics Screen

When the Graphics screen is active, you can scroll the entire graph-and-axes up, down, right, or left by pressing the appropriate cursor-movement key. Scrolling allows you to see different sections of your graph that are not necessarily visible within the initial graphing window. You can scroll either built-in or user-generated graphs. You cannot scroll when the TRACE feature is active.

Try scrolling the built-in graph of the natural logarithm function in each of the four directions. First press $\boxed{\text{Graph}}$ $\boxed{\text{ln}}$ $\boxed{\text{EXE}}$ to produce the graph (see Fig. 1.6). Then press each of the cursor-movement keys to scroll the graph in all directions.

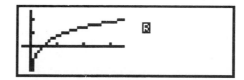

Figure 1.6   The graph of $y = \ln x$ in the viewing window [-0.5, 7.1] by [-1.8, 2.6].

Built-in functions, like the one graphed in Figure 1.6, have different built-in Range settings from those provided on the other models of Casio graphing calculators, which have larger Graphics screens with more pixels than the fx-6300G. For further details on using Casio graphing calculators to solve mathematical problems, read Chapter 5 of the *Graphing Calculator and Computer Graphing Laboratory Manual*. For information on the Casio fx-6300G specifically, refer to the *Owner's Manual* that comes with the calculator.

2

Graphing with the HP 48G

This chapter introduces the graphing and solving capabilities of the HP 48G and HP 48GX graphing-symbolic calculators. The two models differ primarily in that the HP 48GX has more random access memory (RAM) (128K RAM vs. 32K RAM for the 48G) and has two expansion ports for additional RAM or read-only memory (ROM). In this chapter, both calculators are referred to as the HP 48G.

Like its predecessors, the HP 48S and HP 48SX, the HP 48G is a sophisticated, general purpose, mathematics calculator. Unlike its predecessors, however, the HP 48G does not require a much larger learning-time investment than other calculators on the market. This is because of its extensive use of pull-down menus and options and on-screen prompts.

Before reading the rest of this chapter, you are encouraged to read sections 9.1.2—9.1.5 of the *Graphing Calculator and Computer Graphing Laboratory Manual* for information regarding reverse Polish notation (RPN), stack operations, and variables. The calculator's flexibility and many built-in functions make it difficult to "give" a complete picture of its possible applications. Therefore you are also encouraged to read the appropriate chapters in the owner's manual that comes with the calculator.

2.1 _____ HP 48G Fundamentals

2.1.1 Using the Multipurpose ON Key

Press ON to turn on your calculator. This key not only turns the HP 48G on but also acts as a **general purpose interruption key** (note the word CANCEL written below the key). It halts calculator execution and returns to a previous state. For example, when you are entering a number, pressing ON clears the number and returns to the previous stack display.

Any time the calculator is in a state you want to abandon, press $\boxed{\text{ON}}$ one or more times, and it will eventually return to its default state, showing the stack. If the calculator beeps and shows an error message, press $\boxed{\text{ON}}$ to remove the message.

Press $\boxed{\rightarrow}$ $\boxed{\text{OFF}}$ to turn off the calculator. The $\boxed{\text{OFF}}$ key is a **shifted** version of the $\boxed{\text{ON}}$ key (the green $\boxed{\rightarrow}$ key).

2.1.2 Adjusting the Display contrast

With the calculator on, hold down $\boxed{\text{ON}}$ and press $\boxed{+}$ to darken or $\boxed{-}$ to lighten the display.

2.1.3 Exploring the HP 48G Keyboard

Each of the 49 keys on the HP 48G performs more than one function. A key's primary function is printed in white on the key itself. Simply pressing a key activates this function. A key's other functions are printed above the key in green and/or purple. To access these functions, press the purple $\boxed{\leftarrow}$ or the green $\boxed{\rightarrow}$ before pressing the key. For example, press

$$\boxed{\rightarrow} \quad \boxed{\text{PLOT}}$$

to activate the PLOT application. Finally, a key's alphabetic function, if any, is printed in white below and to the right of the key and is accessed using $\boxed{\alpha}$ (Alpha–Shift). For example, to type an uppercase X on the screen, press

$$\boxed{\alpha} \ \boxed{1/x} \ .$$

A lowercase letter can be accessed by pressing $\boxed{\alpha}$ $\boxed{\leftarrow}$ before entering the letter.

The exceptions to these rules are the menu keys, which are the blank, white keys in the top row of the keyboard. Although these keys do have fixed alphabetic functions (A–F), their other functions vary from application to application. For example, pressing $\boxed{\text{MTH}}$ displays the first six labels shown in (Fig. 2.1), while the second set of labels is made visible via $\boxed{\text{NXT}}$ (see Fig. 2.2).

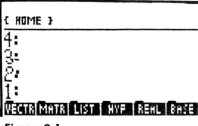

Figure 2.1

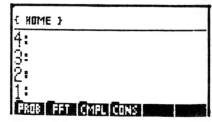

Figure 2.2

Notice that each of these labels has a small tab at the top left corner. This signifies they are file folders that contain other options and/or other file folders. To continue our current example, pressing [B:MATR] activates the MATR folder containing folders and options for matrices, as shown in Fig. 2.3 on page 7.

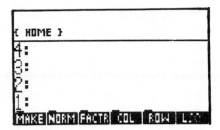

Figure 2.3

These new folders contain options such as the LSQ option as well as other file folders such as the COL folder that contains even more options (→COL, COL→, COL+, etc). Finally, note that on the keyboard the major applications, such as PLOT and SOLVE, are all grouped together and associated with the numerical keys 1–9.

2.2 _____ Learning the Graphing Essentials

The HP 48G makes extensive use of pull-down menus and on-screen prompts; so many of its operational procedures are self-explanatory. Therefore this section is devoted mainly to examples that illustrate the HP 48G's wide range of graphing capabilities.

2.2.1 The Plot Application

To demonstrate this application we will start with a simple example: graphing the function

$$Y = \sin (X).$$

Press

to activate the PLOT menu as shown in Fig. 2.4.

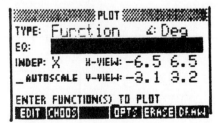

Figure 2.4

Notice the on-screen prompt that reads 'ENTER FUNCTION(S) TO PLOT' as well as the highlight bar positioned to the right of 'EQ:'. *EQ* is a reserved variable that contains a list of the functions to be plotted. Notice also the option labels at the bottom of the screen. The

Edit option, [A:EDIT] allows you to edit the current (in this case, empty) expression; the Choos option, [B:CHOOS] allows you to choose an expression or list from among those that are currently saved in user memory. In our next example, we demonstrate how to save an expression more permanently in user memory; in this example, we will simply save our expression temporarily in the variable *EQ*. Press [A:EDIT] to place an insert cursor between two tick marks on the screen's command line (see Fig. 2.5). The tick marks, ´ ´, are used to begin and end any algebraic object. To enter our expression, press

$$\boxed{\text{SIN}} \quad \boxed{\alpha} \quad \boxed{\text{X}}$$

(see Fig. 2.6) and then press $\boxed{\text{ENTER}}$. The highlight bar then moves to the next option, the independent variable (INDEP), and the on-screen prompt changes to ´ENTER INDEPENDENT VAR(iable) NAME´ (see Fig. 2.7).

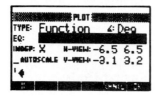

Figure 2.5

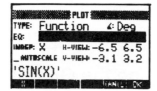

Figure 2.6

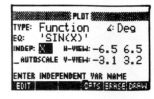

Figure 2.7

The cursor-movement keys move the highlight bar to any option on the PLOT menu. For example, to change the angle units from degrees to radians, press

$$\boxed{\blacktriangleleft} \quad \boxed{\blacktriangleleft} \quad [\text{B:CHOOS}] \quad \boxed{\blacktriangledown} \quad \boxed{\text{ENTER}}.$$

See Figs. 2.8–2.10.

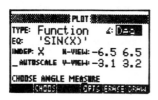

Figure 2.8

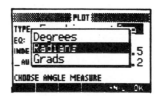

Figure 2.9

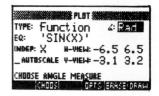

Figure 2.10

Press [E:ERASE] and [F:DRAW] to see the plot (Fig. 2.11).

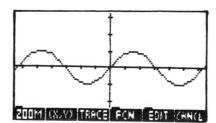

Figure 2.11

2.2.2   The Interactive Plot Mode

Once a graph is plotted, the calculator does not return to the stack; instead it enters what is called the Interactive Plot mode, which allows the user to explore and add graphical elements to the plot. While in this mode, the keyboard is redefined for graphical purposes, as follows:

1. The cursor-movement keys ◀ ▲ ▼ ▶ move the cursor in the indicated direction. Preceding a cursor key with → moves the cursor to the edge of the screen in the indicated direction.

2. − removes the folder/option labels so that all of the Graph screen is visible. This is a toggle key, so pressing it again will retrieve the labels.

3. + displays the cursor coordinates. It also is a toggle key.

4. ← CLEAR erases the plotted graph from the screen, it does not, however, erase the cursor, which remains active. To recover the graph, press

    ON [F:DRAW].

5. ENTER places the cursor coordinates on the stack.

2.2.3   Tracing

As you can see from the labels, the HP 48G has a TRACE feature. To activate this feature, press

[C:TRACE].

Notice that a small highlighted square appears on the TRACE folder label (see Fig. 2.12). Press

[B:(X,Y)]

and use ◀ and ▶ to move the cursor along the curve (see Fig. 2.13). To retrieve the labels, press any menu key. To de-activate the TRACE feature, press [C:TRACE] again. Note that the highlighted square disappears as shown in Fig. 2.14.

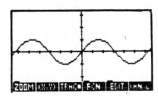
Figure 2.12

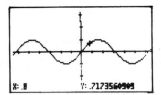
Figure 2.13

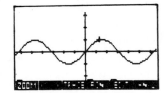
Figure 2.14

2.2.4   Zooming

To continue our example, press

[A:ZOOM]

to access the extensive zoom capabilities of the HP 48G. To change both the horizontal and vertical zoom factors to 5 press

[A:ZFACT] **5** ENTER **5** ENTER [F:OK]

(see Fig. 2.15). Press

[F:OK] [C:ZIN]

to zoom-in by a factor of 5, as shown in Fig. 2.16.

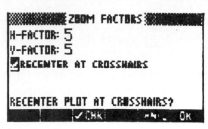

Figure 2.15

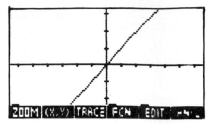

Figure 2.16

Before proceeding, zoom-out again to the default settings by pressing

[A:ZOOM] [D:ZOUT].

One option in the ZOOM folder is the ZTrig option. Press

[A:ZOOM] NXT NXT [C:ZTRIG]

(see Fig. 2.17).
With our original expression and the default plot parameters, the ZTrig option sets the horizontal step to $\pi/20$. Press

[C:TRACE] [B:(X,Y)]

and press ten times to display the value of SIN(X) when $x = \pi/2$ (see Fig. 2.18).

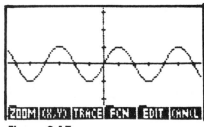

Figure 2.17

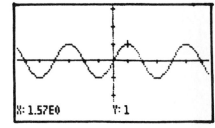

Figure 2.18

You are encouraged to take time to explore all the options in the ZOOM folder. For example, you can zoom-in or out, horizontally and/or vertically to any preset factor. In addition, you can zoom so that the Trace cursor moves through integer abscissas using the ZIntg option or by tenths, using the ZDeci option, effectively creating "friendly windows." And you can always return to the default plotting windows by using the ZDflt option.

Two of the most useful options are the ZSqr option, which changes the range so that the scale on each axis is the same, and the Boxz option, which allows the user to pick a rectangular area that then becomes the viewing window. To return to our example, press any menu key to retrieve the labels, then press

[A:ZOOM] [E:ZSQR]

(see Fig. 2.19). Press

$$[\text{B:(X,Y)}] \; \blacktriangleright$$

to move the cursor along the *x*-axis until you reach $x = \pi/2 \approx 1.57\text{E}0$. Next press $\blacktriangle$ to move the cursor up until it lies directly across from the first tick mark on the *y*-axis. Doing this enables you to see that the cursor, the first tick marks on each axis, and the origin are indeed the vertices of a square (see Fig. 2.20).

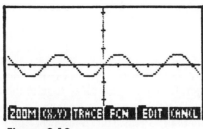

Figure 2.19

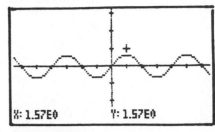

Figure 2.20

To zoom in on this square, press any menu key to retrieve the labels, then press

$$[\text{A:ZOOM}] \;\; [\text{B:BOXZ}] \; .$$

$(\pi/2, \pi/2)$ has already been established as one corner of the viewing window. Move the cursor down to the *x*-axis. Notice that a vertical segment follows the cursor. Next, move the cursor left towards the origin (see Fig. 2.21). Notice the zoom box is beginning to form. Continue moving the cursor until it is positioned at the origin, then press

$$[\text{F:ZOOM}]$$

to obtain the display shown in Fig. 2.22. Notice that the square has been stretched horizontally to fit the rectangular viewing window.

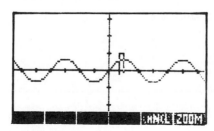

Figure 2.21

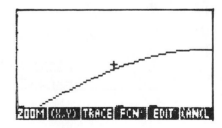

Figure 2.22

2.3 _____ Additional Graphing Capabilities

The following sections, although not an exhaustive accounting of all of the HP 48G's graphing capabilities, will give you a working familiarity with some of the many features. Before continuing, press

to reset the plot window to its default settings.

2.3.1   Using the Catalog

As mentioned before, you can store an expression, equation, or list in the reserved variable *EQ* on a temporary basis only. If the expression in *EQ* is changed, the old expression is overwritten and lost to the user. Often, it is useful to look at the plots of several functions at once or to store one or more functions more permanently. Suppose you want to look at the plots of both $x \cdot \sin(x)$ and $\cos(x)$. Press $\boxed{\text{ON}}$ to exit the Interactive Plot mode and use the cursor-movement keys to move the highlight bar to the current equation (*EQ*). Press

$$[\text{B:CHOOS}]$$

to see a display like that shown in Fig. 2.23. You may have other objects in memory, so your display may not match the one pictured exactly.

Figure 2.23

Press

$$[\text{D:NEW}]$$

(see Fig. 2.24). To enter the first expression 'X*SIN(X)', press

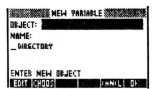

Figure 2.24

and give it the name 'F' by pressing

$$\boxed{\alpha} \quad \boxed{F} \quad \boxed{\text{ENTER}}$$

(see Fig. 2.25). Press [F:OK] to place this new function at the top of the catalog (see Fig. 2.26).

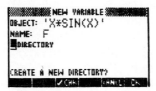

Figure 2.25

Figure 2.26

Follow the same process to place 'COS(X)' in the catalog under the name 'G'. Press

$$[\text{D:NEW}] \quad \boxed{'} \quad \boxed{\text{COS}} \quad \boxed{\alpha} \quad \boxed{X} \quad \boxed{\text{ENTER}} \quad \boxed{\alpha} \quad \boxed{G} \quad \boxed{\text{ENTER}} \quad [\text{F:OK}]$$

(see Fig. 2.27).

Figure 2.27

To plot both of these functions, press

$$[\text{C:}\sqrt{\text{CHK}}]$$

to place a check mark next to the function 'G'; then press

$$\boxed{\blacktriangledown} \quad [\text{C:}\sqrt{\text{CHK}}]$$

to move the highlight bar down 'F' and check it (see Fig. 2.28). Press

$$[\text{F:OK}]$$

to accept your choices. Note that *EQ* is now a list containing the two functions *F* and *G*. Also, note that our original expression, 'SIN(X)', which had been in *EQ*, has been dropped. It is no longer in memory (see Fig. 2.29). On the other hand, if we were to place another function in *EQ*, *F* and *G* would still be in the catalog list, accessed by the Choose option. Press [E:ERASE] [F:DRAW] to see the plots (see Fig. 2.30).

Figure 2.28

Figure 2.29

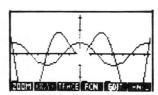

Figure 2.30

In this example, the plots were drawn sequentially. To draw the plots simultaneously, press

$$\boxed{\text{ON}} \quad [\text{D:OPTS}]$$

to reach the PLOT OPTIONS menu. Move the highlight bar to 'SIMULT' and press [C:√CHK] to activate this option (see Fig. 2.31), followed by [F:OK] to return to the main PLOT menu. Then press [E:ERASE] [F:DRAW] to redraw the plots simultaneously.

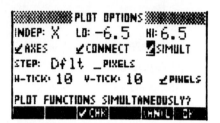

Figure 2.31

2.3.2   The Function Folder

To continue our example, press

$$[\text{D:FCN}]$$

to see the options available in the FCN (functions) folder (see Fig. 2.32). Press $\boxed{\text{NXT}}$ to see the rest of the options (see Fig. 2.33). Most of the options in this folder are concerned with characteristics of the graphs of functions.

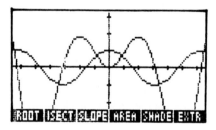

Figure 2.32

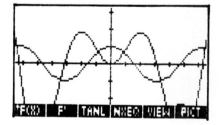

Figure 2.33

Because the first function in the list presently in *EQ* is cos(*x*), pressing

$$\boxed{\text{NXT}} \quad [\text{A:ROOT}]$$

will find a root of y = cos(*x*) that lies nearest to the cursor, which is now at its default location at (0,0). The cursor moves to the root, and the bottom line of the screen flashes the message ´SIGN REVERSAL´ to indicate that the solution was estimated within the limits of the machine. The bottom line then displays the root value 1.57079632679, which is approximately equal to $\pi/2$ (see Fig. 2.34). Press any menu key to restore the option labels.

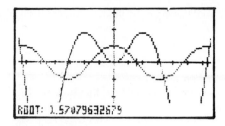

Figure 2.34

You can switch to the other function, 'X∗SIN(X)', by pressing [NXT] to retrieve the rest of the Fcn options as shown in Fig. 2.35, then press

$$[D:NXEQ].$$

The bottom line of the screen now displays the expression ´X∗SIN(X)´ and the cursor jumps vertically to the plot of the new function (see Fig. 2.36). Press any menu key to restore the labels.

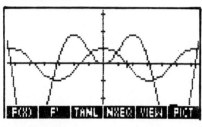

Figure 2.35

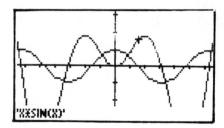

Figure 2.36

To find the root of $x \cdot \sin(x)$ near $x = 3$. Press [+] [+] to see the coordinates, then move the cursor near $x = 3$, and press any menu key followed by

$$[NXT] [A:ROOT],$$

and see 'ROOT:3.14159265359', which is approximately equal to π (see Fig. 2.37).

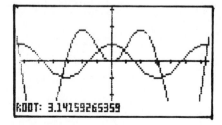

Figure 2.37

Again, press any menu key to restore the labels.

To locate the nearest intersection of the two plots at (3.42561845948, -.9599350991) press

+   [B:ISECT]

(see Fig 2.38).

Again, the sign reversal message flashes briefly, announcing that the solution is an approximation. The values of the roots and the intersections of the plots are all placed on the stack automatically. Press ON repeatedly until you return to the stack (see Fig. 2.39, your menu label may differ).

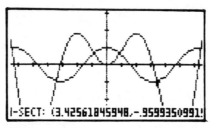

Figure 2.38

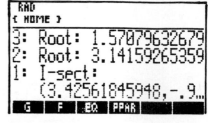

Figure 2.39

Return to the Interactive Plot mode and FCN folder by pressing

→   PLOT   [F:DRAW] [D:FCN].

Then press

NXT   [D:NXEQ]

to return to the cosine function, and then press any menu key to retrieve the menu labels NXT [F:EXTR] to find the nearest maximum or minimum of the current function, in our case the maximum of 1 for cos(x) at x = 0 (see Fig. 2.40).

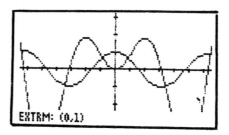

Figure 2.40

2.4 _____ Polar Graphing

Thanks to the pull-down menus, polar graphing on the HP 48G is easier than it was on the HP 48S. Press [ON] to return to the PLOT application, then press [▲] to move the highlight bar to the equation 'TYPE' and press [B:CHOOS] to see the list of options. Use the cursor-movement keys to highlight 'Polar' and press [ENTER].

EXAMPLE 1

Problem Graph the limacon $r = 1.5(1 - 2\cos\theta)$.
Solution Move the highlight bar to the current equation, by pressing [▼]. Press

to obtain 'Y = 1.5*(1−2*COS(X))' as the equation *EQ*. Because the default interval for θ is $[0, 2\pi]$, press

[E:ERASE] [F:DRAW]

to see the plot. Press [−] to remove the labels (see Fig. 2.41).

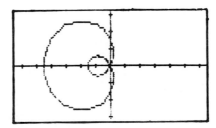

Figure 2.41

2.5 _____ Parametric Graphing

As with polar graphing, pull-down menus have simplified the plotting of parametric graphs.

EXAMPLE 2

Problem Graph the Lissajous figure $x = 3\sin(3t)$, $y = 2\sin(4t)$ for $0 \le t \le 6.5$.
Solution Press [ON] to leave the Interactive Plot mode and return to the PLOT application, then use the cursor-movement keys to move the highlight bar to 'TYPE'. Press

[B:CHOOS],

use the cursor-movement keys to move the highlight bar to 'Parametric' and press ⏍ENTER⏍ (see Fig. 2.42).

Figure 2.42

The equation must be entered in the form ($x(t)$, $y(t)$).Move the highlight bar to 'EQ' and press

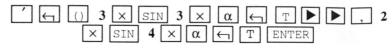

to obtain

'(3*SIN(3*t), 2*SIN(4*t)'.

Your screen will not show the entirety of this object. Change the independent variable to 't' by selecting 'INDEP' and pressing

⏍α⏍ ⏍←⏍ ⏍T⏍ [F:OK].

Press

[E:ERASE] [F:DRAW]

to see the plot (see Fig. 2.43).

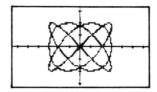

Figure 2.43

2.6 _____ Conclusion

The foregoing sections have described only a fraction of the capabilities of the HP 48G. In addition to the catalog of user-defined functions, there is an Equation Library in ROM that is accessed by pressing ⏍→⏍ ⏍EQ LIB⏍. Equations in this library are grouped by topic name. When it is advantageous, the equations have accompanying diagrams to identify the variables. There also is an extensive UNITS application, where values can be tagged with units. The HP 48G then keeps track of the units and changes them appropriately as calculations are made. An extensive STAT (statistical) application is also available, as well as a SYMBOLIC application, which allows the user to do everything from symbolic differentiation to symbolic manipulation of an algebraic expression. Finally, the HP 48G can print graphs, etc., to a thermal printer via the infrared Input/Output port (like using your TV remote control). The I/O port also can be used to transfer programs and any other information (like matrices) from one HP 48 to another. Cables also are available that will allow you to transfer files to and from either a PC-compatible or a Macintosh computer. The owner's manual contains information on all of these topics.

CHAPTER 3

Graphing with the Sharp EL-9200C and EL-9300C

The Sharp EL-9200C and EL-9300C calculators are versatile, powerful tools that offer students an extremely wide range of functionality in a user-friendly format. Both utilize almost identical software that includes the following features:

- Rectangular, Polar, and Parametric graphing
- Programming
- Statistical computing
- Statistical graphing
- Matrix operations
- Complex number calculation
- Numerical calculus

Both also include a large, high-contrast screen and a hard case for protection when it's not in use. In addition the EL-9300C offers a powerful Solver mode, 32K of RAM, a communications port, and a back-up battery.

The instructions in this chapter apply to both Sharp calculators, except the discussion of the Solver mode, which applies only to the EL-9300. Section 3.1 discusses the keypad and some of the calculators' major features and functions, while Section 3.2 introduces graphing techniques. Section 3.3 addresses the Solver. There are many additional features beyond those we describe here. The best way to explore the calculator is to look inside the menus to see the available options and experiment with them. You also are urged to use the *Owner's Manual and Solutions Handbook* that came with your calculator for more information on how to use the machine.

Each calculator has a built-in self-demonstration program. To use this program, follow the steps on page 22.

To start the demonstration,

1. when the calculator is turned off, press *and hold* $\boxed{\text{ENTER}}$ and
2. press $\boxed{\text{ON}}$.

To pause the demonstration, press $\boxed{\text{ENTER}}$.
To restart the demonstration, press $\boxed{\text{ENTER}}$.
To exit the demonstration, press $\boxed{\text{ON}}$.

3.1 ⸺ Getting Started on the EL-9200C and EL-9300C

The front of the calculator can be divided into two sections: the viewing screen in the upper third and the keys in the lower two thirds. Next, we discuss the keypad.

3.1.1   Exploring the Keypad

The major key groups occupy the top six rows. Each key has a primary function whose name or symbol is printed in white on the key. Most keys also have a second function and alphabetic function whose name or symbol is printed above the keys.

You can access the second functions printed in yellow by pressing $\boxed{\text{2ndF}}$ and then the desired key desired. For example, to access $\boxed{\sin^{-1}}$, do the following:

1. Press $\boxed{\text{2ndF}}$.
2. Press $\boxed{\sin^{-1}}$.

To access the alphabetic functions printed in blue above the keys, do the following:

1. press $\boxed{\text{ALPHA}}$ and
2. press the desired key.

To lock the calculator into Alpha mode, press $\boxed{\text{2ndF}}$ $\boxed{\text{A-LOCK}}$.
To clear the Alpha lock, press $\boxed{\text{ALPHA}}$. Indicators at the top of the screen tell whether $\boxed{\text{ALPHA}}$ or $\boxed{\text{2ndF}}$ has been pressed.
The keypad is divided into parts according to key position, as follows:

- Row 1 - the **Operation mode keys**. Used to choose the mode in which you want to work. From left to right, they are as follows:
  - Calculation mode

  - Graphing mode

  - Programming mode

  - Statistics mode

Two additional modes are available as second functions:

- Solver mode (EL-9300C only)

- Statistical graph mode

To access any mode, press the appropriate mode key or keys.

- Row 2 - the **Graph function keys**. Used to access the various operations in the Graphing mode.
- Row 3 - the **Menu keys**. Used to access menus associated with functions and operations not available directly from the key pad (see Section 3.1.2 for information on how to work with these menus).
- Row 4 - the **Control** and **Editing keys** . Used to control the operation of the calculator (SET UP)and to edit expressions and equations entered in the calculator (DEL , 2ndF INS , BS (backspace), CL (clear), and 2ndF CA (clear all)).
- Rows 5—10–the **Function** and **Arithmetic keys** are similar to those on any scientific or graphing calculator. The popular X/θ/T is located on the right-hand side, just above the) When pressed, this key displays an X, θ, or T, depending on the graph coordinate system selected in the SET UP menu.

3.1.2 Operating the Menus

Many operations and functions on these calculators are accessed through a two-level menu system. All of the menus work in the same manner. The two used most often are the MATH and MENU menus. Following is a summary of what the various menus do:

- MATH menu
  Offers all the additional functions available for the current mode (see Fig. 3.1). (Functions not available will display a row of dots instead of the function.) For each available function, you can access a submenu of additional operations available for that function in the selected mode.

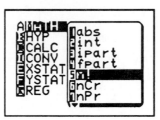

Figure 3.1

- MENU menu
  Contains all of the additional operations and submodes available for the currently selected mode.

- COMMAND menu
  Used only in the Programming mode. It contains all of the programming commands.
- OPTION menu
  Used to adjust the contrast and manage the memory. In addition, for the EL-9300C, you use it to operate the calculator's communication link to a printer, another EL-9300C, an overhead display unit or a cassette player.

To exit from the currently displayed menu and save your current selections, press

$$\boxed{\text{QUIT}}.$$

There are two ways to make menu selections:

1. Use the cursor-movement keys. As you scroll through the menu, items on the menu are highlighted. When the menu item you want is highlighted, press $\boxed{\blacktriangleright}$ or $\boxed{\text{ENTER}}$ to move the cursor into the submenu (if there is one). Then use $\boxed{\blacktriangle}$ and $\boxed{\blacktriangledown}$ to highlight and $\boxed{\text{ENTER}}$ to select your choice from the submenu.
2. Use the letter and number keys to make quick selections.
   a. To select from the main menu, press the letter corresponding to the menu item you want.

Note: You don't have to press $\boxed{\text{ALPHA}}$ *first in this case.*

   b. To select from the submenu, press the number of your submenu selection.

3.1.3   Using the Equation Editor

The Equation Editor helps make expressions easier to see and understand by enabling you to enter and edit equations and expressions and then view them in the format in which they would appear on paper. It is the default editor on both calculators and is used in the Calculator, Graphing, and Solver modes.

A traditional "one line" editor also is available, which will make the calculator operate similar to Casio and Texas Instruments graphing calculators. To turn on this feature, press

$$\boxed{\text{SET UP}}\ [\text{F:EDIT}]\ [\text{2:ONE LINE}].$$

The remainder of these instructions assume the calculator is set to the Equation Editor.

Expressions are entered as they are on any other graphing or programmable calculator, except that the expression appears in two dimensions (up/down and left/right) or (more than one line) or both. The following conventions apply:

- To exit from multi-line functions such as exponents and roots or out of a denominator, press $\boxed{\blacktriangleright}$.
- All cursor-movement keys can be used to move around an expression. However, to return quickly to the beginning or end of an expression, press $\boxed{\text{2ndF}}\ \boxed{\blacktriangleleft}$ or $\boxed{\text{2ndF}}\ \boxed{\blacktriangleright}$, respectively.
- To cause the calculator to compute an expression, press $\boxed{\text{ENTER}}$.

Note: It isn't necessary to be at the end of an expression when you press $\boxed{\text{ENTER}}$.

Figure 3.2 shows an example equation as it was entered in the calculator (lines one and two) and as it was edited (line 3).

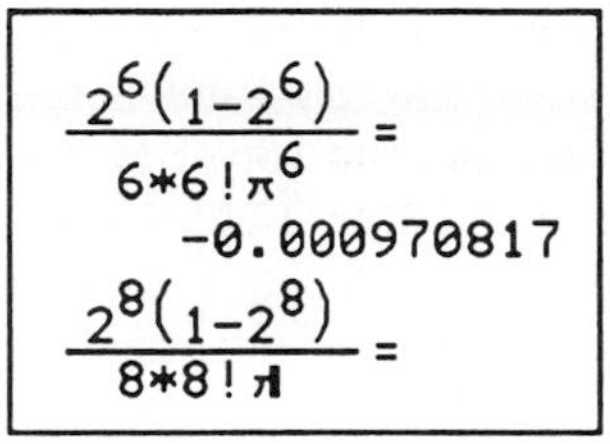

$$\frac{2^6\left(1-2^6\right)}{6*6!\,\pi^6} =$$
$$-0.000970817$$
$$\frac{2^8\left(1-2^8\right)}{8*8!\,\pi} =$$

Figure 3.2

3.1.4 Entering Data in Fields

In many cases, data must be entered into a field; for example, statistical, matrix, or graph range data. Numbers, variables, and expressions can be entered in any field; however, only the final calculated values are stored. Further, calculations also can be performed on a field.

In an example using the RANGE feature, do the following:

1. Enter this feature by pressing the Graph key and `RANGE` .

The x Range screen appears, as shown in Fig. 3.3.

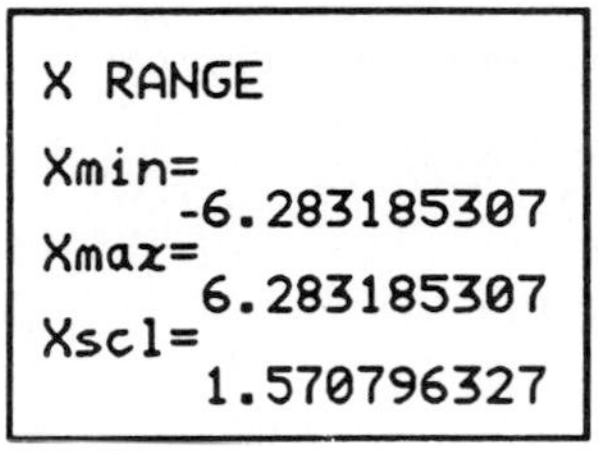

X RANGE
Xmin=
$\qquad$ -6.283185307
Xmax=
$\qquad$ 6.283185307
Xscl=
$\qquad$ 1.570796327

Figure 3.3

To change a field value,

1. use the cursor-movement keys to move to the Range you want to change, in this case, the *x*Min field,
2. type the new value, for example, 3.5, and
3. press `ENTER`.

The new value, 3.5, replaces the old value.

To perform a calculation on a field, for example, to double the Range value of 3.5,

1. reposition the cursor on the *x*Min field,
2. press `×` 2 , and
3. press `ENTER` .

The old value, 3.5, is replaced with the new value, 7.0 (that is, the result of 2 times 3.5).

If you make an error while entering data into a field, press `CL` to restore the original value.

3.1.5   Working with Memories and Variables

There are 27 global memories available: the 26 letters of the alphabet (A–Z) and θ. You can access values stored in these memories from any mode. The values entered are stored, even when the calculator is turned off, until you replace them with different values. In Programming and Solver modes, the memories operate as variables.

Lowercase variables are also available. These exist only for the specific program or equation in which they are entered, and their values are not saved after you change modes. To access lowercase variables, do the following:

1. Press 2ndF .
2. Press the letter desired.

Lowercase variables can be strung together with numbers to form an unlimited number of possible variables. They are useful in the Programming mode to avoid accidental overwriting of the Global variables. Examples of calculator memories are A, X, and θ; examples of variables are *A, X,*θ, and area.

3.1.6   Configuring the Calculator

The general configuration of the calculator is controlled through the SET UP menu. To access this menu, press SET UP . Change the settings just as you make selections in other menus. For example, to select degrees, do the following:

1. Press SET UP

The SET UP menu is displayed (see Fig. 3.4).

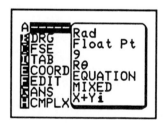

Figure 3.4

2. Press [B:DRG] and then [1:Deg] .
3. Press ENTER to leave the menu.

3.1.7   Working with the Calculation Mode

Submodes.   There are four submodes of the Calculation mode, as follows:

- Real (the default)
- Nbase
  Allows hexadecimal, octal, and binary calculations and conversions.
- Matrix

- Complex

    To change modes, do the following:

1. Press ⃞MENU⃞.

The MODE menu appears, as shown in Fig. 3.5.

Figure 3.5

2. Press the number that corresponds to the mode you want.

You are returned to the Calculation screen in the selected mode.

Playback.   In the Calculation mode, many past equations entered in the calculator can be recalled. The last 100 keystrokes are stored in playback memory.

- To recall the most recent expression, press ⃞▲⃞ .
- To recall expressions earlier than the most recent, press ⃞2ndF⃞ ⃞▲⃞ .

    Repeat this sequence to step backward to previous expressions (up to the 100 keystroke limit).

EXAMPLE 1   Playback

Problem Evaluate $\dfrac{\sin X}{X-1}$ for values of $X = $ -1, 0, and 1.

Solution Follow these steps:

1. Press the Calculation key to enter the Calculation mode.
2. Press ⃞MENU⃞ [1:REAL] to put the calculator in Real mode (if not already there).
3. Store the value of -1 into X by entering the following key sequence:

$$⃞(-)⃞ \quad 1 \quad ⃞STO⃞ \quad ⃞X/\theta/T⃞$$

4. Press ⃞ᵃ/b⃞ so you can enter a fraction.
5. Press ⃞▲⃞ ⃞BS⃞ to clear the ANS command.
6. Enter the expression by keying in the following sequence:

$$⃞sin⃞ \quad ⃞X/\theta/T⃞ \quad ⃞▶⃞ \quad ⃞X/\theta/T⃞ \quad ⃞-⃞ \quad 1$$

7. Press ⃞ENTER⃞ to calculate the equation.

The result, 0.420735492, is calculated (see Fig. 3.6).

To store 0 in *X*, do the following:

1. Enter the following key sequence:

$$0 \quad \boxed{\text{STO}} \quad \boxed{\text{X}/\theta/\text{T}}$$

2. Recall the equation and recalculate the expression by entering the following sequence:

$$\boxed{\blacktriangle} \quad \boxed{\text{2ndF}} \quad \boxed{\blacktriangle} \quad \boxed{\text{ENTER}}$$

The answer for 0 is calculated.

To store 1 in *X*, do the following:

1. Enter the following key sequence:

$$1 \quad \boxed{\text{STO}} \quad \boxed{\text{X}/\theta/\text{T}}$$

2. Recall the equation and recalculate the expression by entering the following sequence:

$$\boxed{\blacktriangle} \quad \boxed{\text{2ndF}} \quad \boxed{\blacktriangle} \quad \boxed{\text{ENTER}}$$

The calculator responds with an error message (see Fig. 3.7) because you are trying to divide by zero. There is no real-number value for $\frac{\sin X}{X-1}$ for X = 1.

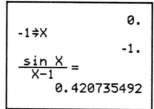

Figure 3.6

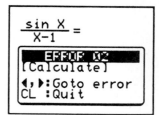

Figure 3.7

3.2 _____ Graphing with the EL-9200C and EL-9300C

3.2.1 Graphing and Tracing Multiple Functions

You can graph and trace up to four functions simultaneously. To do this, you first enter the equations for each function on the Equation screen. These four functional expressions are labeled Y1, Y2, Y3, and Y4. Example 2 explains how to enter equations.

The following conventions apply:

- To move from one expression to another, press $\boxed{\text{2ndF}}$ and either $\boxed{\blacktriangle}$ or $\boxed{\blacktriangledown}$ (depending on which expression you want to reach).

- After you enter the fourth expression, a Fill screen appears, on which you can indicate if you want to shade above or below Y1 through Y4.
- To return to the Equation screen from any other Graph screen, press $\boxed{\text{EQTN}}$.

Example 2   Using the Equation Menu

Problem Graph $\dfrac{\sin X}{X-1}$ and $\dfrac{1}{X-1}$.

Solution To graph these two equations, do the following:

1. Press the Graph key to enter the Graph mode.

The screen displays 'Y1 ='. (Press $\boxed{\text{CL}}$ if any other equation is showing).

2. Enter the first equation by keying in the following sequence:

$$\boxed{^a/_b} \quad \boxed{\text{sin}} \quad \boxed{\text{X}/\theta/\text{T}} \quad \boxed{\blacktriangleright} \quad \boxed{\text{X}/\theta/\text{T}} \quad \boxed{-} \quad 1$$

3. Press $\boxed{\text{ENTER}}$ (see Fig. 3.8).

The equation is stored; the screen clears the first equation, and displays 'Y2 ='.

4. Enter the second equation by keying in the following sequence:

$$1 \quad \boxed{^a/_b} \quad \boxed{\text{X}/\theta/\text{T}} \quad \boxed{-} \quad 1$$

5. Press $\boxed{\text{ENTER}}$.

The equation is stored; the screen clears the second equation, and displays 'Y3 ='.

   If you want to graph more equations, enter them as Y3 and Y4.

   Before drawing the graph, you must set the Range (also called the viewing rectangle or window). How to do this is explained in Section 3.2.2. For illustrative purposes, Example 2 continues for several sections.

3.2.2   Setting the Range and Auto Range

To set the Range values, do the following:

1. Press $\boxed{\text{RANGE}}$.

The screen displays the current values for the x Range (see Fig. 3.9). To display the y Range values, press $\boxed{\blacktriangleleft}$. To redisplay the x Range, press $\boxed{\blacktriangleright}$ again.

```
Y1🔲 sin X
      ────
      X-1
```

Figure 3.8

```
X RANGE

Xmin=
      -6.283185307
Xmax=
       6.283185307
Xscl=
       1.570796327
```

Figure 3.9

2. Either

   a. change the values for the Range, or

   b. press ☐MENU☐ to select from 19 default Ranges available.

Because the equation in Example 2 works with the sine function, choose the default sine Range as follows:

3. Press ☐MENU☐ [D:TRIG] [1: sin, cos].

The calculator automatically sets the x Range values from -2π to 2π and the y Range values from -1.55 to 1.55.

4. Press the Graph key to draw the graph (see Fig. 3.10).

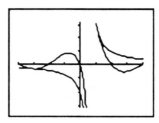

Figure 3.10

   Also available is an AUTO RANGE feature that will automatically set the *y* Range values and then draw the graph. This feature is helpful when a function doesn't appear in the selected Range. To use the AUTO RANGE feature, press

☐2ndF☐ ☐AUTO☐

3.2.3   Drawing the Graph

Several options are available for drawing graphs.

1. When viewing the graph or the equations, press ☐MENU☐.

The menu shown in Fig. 3.11 is displayed.

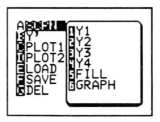

Figure 3.11

2. Select the option you want.
   The options available are as follows:

• SCRN allows you to quickly move between the Equation, Fill, and Graph screens.

- Y′ enables you to turn on a derivative trace. You will learn about derivations if you continue your mathematical studies with a course in calculus.
- PLOT1 allows drawing the graphs with or without connecting the dots.
- PLOT2 allows graphs to be drawn sequentially or simultaneously.
- LOAD, SAVE, and DEL are used to store up to 99 sets of equation titles. When you choose SAVE, the four equations Y1–Y4, the Range values, selected Menu options, and the set-up configuration are stored under one name for future use.

3.2.4 Tracing a Graph

To trace the curve of the graph, do the following:

1. Press either ◀ or ▶ .

The blinking cross cursor appears on the screen (see Fig. 3.12).

2. Continue to press ◀ or ▶ to trace the graph. To move quickly to the right-hand side of the screen, press 2ndF ▶ ; to move quickly to the left-hand side of the screen, press 2ndF ◀ .

As the cursor traces the graph, the x-coordinate of the cursor and the corresponding functional values are given at the bottom of the screen.

3. To move the cursor between the graphs, press ▲ or ▼ .

4. To exit the TRACE feature, press CL .

   Notice that when the cursor moves off the screen, the display scrolls in the x-and y-directions as needed to keep the cursor on the screen.

   You also can obtain a Trace value for the derivative, that is, the slope of the curve at the x-value. This feature uses a numerical method to estimate the derivative at each x-value as you trace along a graph. To do this, press

$$\boxed{\text{MENU}} \quad [\text{B:Y}'] \ [1:\text{ON}]$$

See Fig. 3.13.

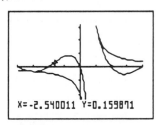

Figure 3.12

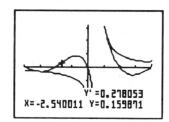

Figure 3.13

3.2.5 Zeroing in on Certain Points

It's easy to focus on certain points of interest using the JUMP feature. To view the options this feature offers, press

$$\boxed{\text{2ndF}} \quad \boxed{\text{JUMP}}$$

The cursor doesn't need to be near the selected point of interest in order for the calculator to find the desired point; the calculator will begin at the cursor position and work to the right looking for the point. If no point is found, the calculator displays the message 'NO SOLUTION IN RANGE.' Note that the TRACE feature need not be active for you to use the JUMP feature.

As an example, find the intersection of the two equations you entered in Section 3.2.1 as follows:

1. Press

$$\boxed{\text{2nd}} \quad \boxed{\text{JUMP}} \quad [1:\text{INTERSECT}] ;$$

where 1 is the Intersect option (see Fig. 3.14).

The calculator shows that the first intersection occurs at the point with coordinates (-4.712388, -0.175058)(see Fig. 3.15).

Figure 3.14

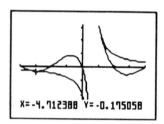

Figure 3.15

2. To find the first maximum of Y_1, press ▲ which places the cursor on Y_1.

3. Enter the following key sequence:

$$\boxed{\text{2ndF}} \quad \boxed{\text{JUMP}} \quad [3:\text{MAX}]$$

The calculator shows that a maximum of 0.424607 occurs at X = -1.132267.

3.2.6   Using ZOOM

To get a closer look at a part of the graph, use the ZOOM feature. To use ZOOM, do the following:

1. Press $\boxed{\text{ZOOM}}$.

The screen displays the ZOOM menu, which is shown in Fig. 3.16.

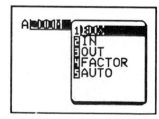

Figure 3.16

2. Press the number of the option desired.

The calculator returns you to the graph and redraws the graph according to the parameters of the option you selected.

Following are the options available:

- BOX
  enables you to draw a box on the graph that will become the new window.
- IN and OUT
  scale the graph by an amount specified by the Zoom factor.
- AUTO
  sets the *y* Range values automatically. This option is the same as 2ndF AUTO .

For example, suppose you want to zoom in on the left part of the two curves. Do the following:

1. Press ZOOM [1:BOX], where 1 is the Box option.
2. Use the cursor-movement keys to mark the first corner of the box.
3. Press ENTER .
4. Hold down the cursor-movement keys to draw the box that will be your new viewing window (see Fig. 3.17).

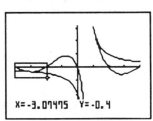

X=-3.07475 Y=-0.4

Figure 3.17

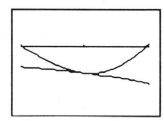

Figure 3.18

5. Press ENTER to redraw the graph.

The graph is redrawn according to the coordinates of the box you drew (see Fig. 3.18).

3.2.7   Working with Polar Graphs

In addition to the Rectangular coordinate system, you can use other coordinate systems such as the Polar coordinate system. To change the graphing system to the Polar coordinate system, enter the following key sequence:

SET UP   [E:COORD] [2:Rθ]

Then press [B:DRG] [2: Rad] to ensure your calculator is in Radian mode.
The following changes occur:

- In Graphing mode, the calculator changes the prompt from Y1 to R1.
- Pressing X/θ/T yields a θ (theta) instead of an *X*.

- The Range screen changes from to include θMin, θMax, and θstep. Note that θMax and θstep are linked; one automatically adjusts after you enter a value for the other.

The TRACE and ZOOM features work in the Polar coordinate system just as they do in the Rectangular coordinate system. Before continuing on to Example 3; change the graphing system to the Rectangular coordinate system.

EXAMPLE 3   Graphing with Polar Coordinates

Problem Graph an eight-petal rose (sin 4 θ with a θ Range of 0 to 2π).
Solution Follow these steps to produce the rose:

1. Enter the following key sequence:

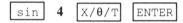

2. To set up a "square" window, press

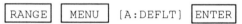

Note: This key sequence will set up a square window in any of the graphing mode options—Rectangular, Polar, and Parametric.

3. To change θMax, to 2π, press:

▼ 2 | 2ndF | | π | | ENTER | | 2ndF | | AUTO |

The result is as shown in Fig. 3.19.

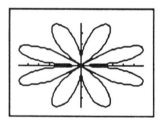

Figure 3.19

3.2.8   Working with Parametric Graphs

Parametric graphs are based on the Rectangular coordinate system, except that *X* and *Y* are individual functions that have *T* as an independent variable. In the Parametric graphing mode, X1T and Y1T replace Y1 as an equation prompt. *t*Max and *t*step are linked; one automatically adjusts after you enter a value for the other.

To change to the Parametric graphing mode, enter the following key sequence:

| SET UP | [E:COORD] [3:XYT] | QUIT |

To ensure you are in Radian mode; press

| SET UP | [B:DRG] [2:RAD] | QUIT | .

EXAMPLE 4   Parametric Graphing

Problem Graph X1T = sin 3*T*, Y1T = cos 5*T* with a *t* Range of 0 to 2π.
Solution Follow these steps to create this graph:

1. To enter the equations, press

    $\boxed{\text{sin}}$ **3** $\boxed{\text{X}/\theta/\text{T}}$ $\boxed{\text{ENTER}}$ $\boxed{\text{cos}}$ **5** $\boxed{\text{X}/\theta/\text{T}}$ $\boxed{\text{ENTER}}$

2. To set the range, press

    $\boxed{\text{RANGE}}$ **0** $\boxed{\text{ENTER}}$ **2** $\boxed{\text{2ndF}}$ $\boxed{\pi}$ $\boxed{\text{ENTER}}$ $\boxed{\text{2ndF}}$ $\boxed{\text{AUTO}}$

    The result is as shown in Fig. 3.20.

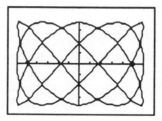

Figure 3.20

3.3 _____ Using Solver to Simplify Problem Solving (EL-9300C only)

The EL-9300 includes a powerful feature called the Solver mode. This mode allows you to solve for any variable in any equation entered. Because there is no need to rearrange the equation to solve for a particular variable, finding solutions is greatly simplified. Equations can be solved using any of three solving methods. To change to Solver mode, press

$\boxed{\text{2ndF}}$ $\boxed{\text{SOLVER}}$

3.3.1 Entering an Equation

Expressions are entered in the Solver mode just as they are in the Calculation mode, except in order to form an equation in the Solver, you must use an equals sign (=) ($\boxed{\text{ALPHA}}$ $\boxed{=}$). To prevent your accidentally overwriting any Global memories, lowercase variables are used (see also Section 3.1.5 for more information on memories and variables). The following conventions apply:

*   To enter a lowercase variable,
    1. press $\boxed{\text{ALPHA}}$ and
    2. enter the letter.
*   To enter an uppercase variable,
    1. press $\boxed{\text{ALPHA}}$ $\boxed{\text{2ndF}}$ and
    2. enter the letter.

- To enter a subscript number,
    1. press $\boxed{\texttt{2ndF}}$ and
    2. enter the number.

Press $\boxed{\texttt{ENTER}}$ after entering your equation.

EXAMPLE 5   Entering Equations in Solver

Problem How long does it take for a ball thrown straight up into the air to reach a height of 10 m? Assume that the person throwing the ball can do so at 20 m/sec and that that person's hand is 2 m high when the ball is released. The force of gravity is 9.88 m/sec^2. Disregard air resistance.

Solution Enter the basic equation of motion as follows:

1. Enter Solver mode by pressing $\boxed{\texttt{2ndF}}$ $\boxed{\texttt{SOLVER}}$

2. Key in the following sequence:

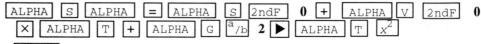

3. $\boxed{\texttt{ENTER}}$

A list of variables is displayed (see Fig. 3.21).

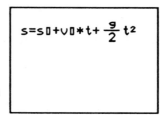

$$s = s_0 + v_0 * t + \frac{g}{2} t^2$$

Figure 3.21

Note: You can return to the equation by pressing $\boxed{\texttt{EQTN}}$.

Observe that the multiplication sign is required between variables so that the calculator does not make 'v₀t' into one variable. For illustrative purposes, Example 5 continues in the next several sections.

3.3.2   Entering the Known Values

Enter all the values except for the single unknown one. Remember you can use the cursor-movement keys to move between the variables. Enter the variables as follows:

1. The height, s, we want the ball to reach is 10, therefore enter

$$\mathbf{1\ 0}\ \boxed{\texttt{ENTER}}$$

2. The initial height, s_0, is 2 m when the ball is released, therefore enter

$$\mathbf{2}\ \boxed{\texttt{ENTER}}$$

3. The initial velocity, v_0, is 20 m/sec, therefore enter **2 0** ENTER .

The results should be as in Fig. 3.22.

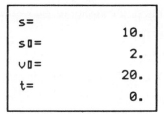

Figure 3.22

As time (t) is what we are solving for, skip it by pressing ▼ . In addition, because the acceleration due to gravity (g) is in the opposite direction of the initial velocity, it must be negative; therefore enter the following key sequence:

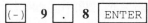

3.3.3   Choosing the Solving Method

To find the unknown variable, you can select from three solving methods. To learn what those are, press

MENU [B:METHOD]

The three methods are displayed in a submenu as follows (see Fig. 3.23):

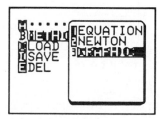

Figure 3.23

- Equation method
  Internally rearranges the variables to solve for the unknown variable. Note that it might not always be able to solve the unknown.

- Newton method
  Uses an initial guess with an iterative approach to approximate the solution.

- Graphic method
  Draws a graph of the right-hand and left-hand sides of the equation in order to find the solution.

For Example 5, we'll use the Graphic method, therefore press [3: GRAPHIC] and the calculator returns you to the previous screen, which shows the values of the variables you entered earlier.

3.3.4   Solving for the Answer

To solve for the unknown variable, do as follows:

1. Move the cursor to the variable, in this case t, using the cursor-movement keys.

2. Press

You must press $\boxed{\text{ENTER}}$ the second time to confirm you want to solve for that variable (see Fig. 3.24).

Next, you need to enter Range values for the Graphic method. We know that the ball must be in the air for some amount of time and that the ball might remain in the air for as long as 5 sec. We use these estimates for the Range by entering the following key sequence:

See Fig. 3.25. The calculator uses the AUTO RANGE feature to draw the graph. The horizontal axis is scaled based on the variable being sought, in this case t, and the vertical axis is, in this case, the height of the ball. The horizontal line represents $s=10$. The curve shows the height of the ball as time passes. We can see that the ball starts a little above ground level, reaches a maximum height, and falls back to the ground.

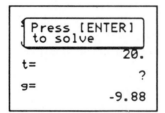

Figure 3.24

Figure 3.25

The calculator then automatically computes the solution, which occurs at the intersection of the two graphs, approximately $t = .45$ sec (see Fig. 3.26).

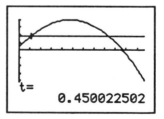

Figure 3.26

3.3.5   Solving for Additional Answers

Viewing the equation graphically, we can see that there is more than one solution. The second solution occurs when the ball falls back to the ground and is again momentarily at a height of 10 m. This solution can be found using the TRACE feature (discussed in Section 3.2.4) to move the cursor to the other solution of the ZOOM feature (discussed in section 3.2.6) to move in on the solution and then trace to measure it. You also can use the JUMP feature by pressing

| 2ndF | | JUMP |

which will cause the calculator to find the second solution, in this case, approximately $t = 3.63$ sec (see Fig. 3.27).

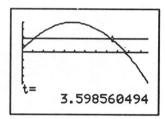

Figure 3.27

3.3.6   Storing Equations

Up to 99 equations used in the Solver mode can be named and stored for later reference. To save an equation, do the following:

1. Press | MENU | [D:SAVE] | ENTER |.
2. Enter a title for the equation.
3. Press | ALPHA | | ENTER |.

    To retrieve a function, do the following:

1. Press | MENU | [C:LOAD] | ENTER |.
2. Arrow down to highlight equation derived.
3. Press | ENTER |.

Chapter 4

The TI-82 Graphing Calculator

The TI-82 is a versatile tool for algebra, trigonometry, and precalculus mathematics. In addition to all the features of a scientific calculator, the TI-82 has large-screen computation and programming capabilities and built-in software for working with graphs, tables, lists, matrices, sequences, probabilities, and statistics. Hence, this calculator is actually a powerful, user-friendly, hand-held computer.

This chapter is designed to familiarize you with many aspects of your calculator. Have your calculator handy so you can work through the examples as you read it. Feel free to explore the menus and features of your calculator. A few hours of productive play can help you reach a comfort level that will help you solve problems using this powerful tool.

4.1 ____ Getting Started on the TI-82

4.1.1 Exploring the Keyboard

Take a minute to study the keys on your TI-82. There are 10 rows of keys, each with five keys, except for the four specially arranged cursor-movement keys. These keys are divided into three zones.

- Row 1
  Used for graphing and table building.
- Rows 2, 3, and 4
  Used for accessing menus and editing.
- Rows 5–10
  Used like those on a scientific calculator.

Thinking in terms of these three zones will help you find keys on your calculator.

4.1.2   Using the Multipurpose [ON] Key

The On key [ON] is in the lower left-hand corner of the keyboard. It is used to do the following:

- Turn on the calculator.
- Interrupt graphing if you want to stop before a graph is completely drawn.
- Interrupt program execution to "break out" of a program. [ON] also is used to turn off the calculator. To do this, press

[2nd] [ON] .

Note that the word OFF is written in blue letters just above [ON] and that the color of the letters matches that of the blue [2nd]. In the future, we will say, "press [2nd] [OFF]."

To prolong the life of the batteries, the TI-82 automatically turns itself off after several minutes have elapsed without any activity on the calculator. To turn on the calculator in these circumstances, press

[ON] .

The calculator will turn on and will return you to the screen on which you were working when it turned itself off.

4.1.3   Adjusting the Screen Contrast

You can adjust the screen contrast as needed, choosing from 10 contrast settings that range from 0 (the lightest) to 9 (the darkest).

To darken the screen,

1. press and release [2nd] and then
2. press and hold [▲].

    To lighten the screen,

1. press and release [2nd] and then
2. press and hold [▼].

    If you find it necessary to set the contrast at 8 or 9, it is probably time to change your batteries. (Your calculator uses four AAA batteries.) If after you change the batteries the screen is too dark, simply adjust the contrast following the steps outlined above.

4.2 _____ Performing Numerical Computation and Editing

4.2.1 Returning to the Home Screen

Computation is done on the Home screen. To help you remember how to get to the Home screen from other screens and menus, remember the sentence, "Quit to go Home." This means that if you get lost in a menu and want to return to the Home screen, press

$$\boxed{\text{2nd}} \; \boxed{\text{QUIT}} \; .$$

($\boxed{\text{QUIT}}$ is the second function of $\boxed{\text{MODE}}$ located to the right of the $\boxed{\text{2nd}}$.) If your calculator does not respond to this command, it is probably busy graphing or running a program. In this case, press

$$\boxed{\text{ON}} \; \text{and then either} \; [\texttt{2:Quit}] \; \text{or} \; \boxed{\text{2nd}} \; \boxed{\text{QUIT}} \; .$$

4.2.2 Performing Calculations

1. To compute $2 + 5 \times 8$, press:

$$2 \; \boxed{+} \; 5 \; \boxed{\times} \; 8 \; \boxed{\text{ENTER}}.$$

Your screen should look like Fig. 4.1.

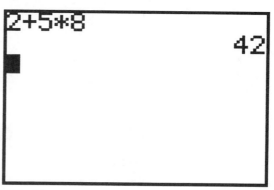

Figure 4.1

2. Find the value of log 100 by pressing

$$\boxed{\text{LOG}} \; \mathbf{100} \; \boxed{\text{ENTER}} \; .$$

Your screen should show the expression and result for both computations (see Fig. 4.2).

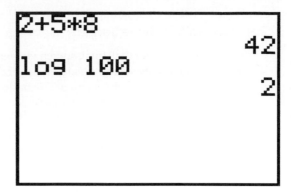

Figure 4.2

Note: *Do not type the letters L, O, and G. The calculator would interpret this as implied multiplication of the variables L, O, and G.*

4.2.3   Working with Error Messages

The TI-82 knows the difference between the binary operation of subtraction (the blue ⎯) and the additive inverse, or "sign change," operation (the gray (-)). To learn how the calculator handles errors related to these keys, let's purposely make a mistake. Enter the following key sequence:

7 ⎣+⎦ ⎣−⎦ 4 ⎣ENTER⎦ .

The calculator should respond as shown in Fig. 4.3. The *error message* indicates you have made a syntax error and have two choices. This ERROR MESSAGE menu is typical of all numbered menus on the TI-82. To select an item from a numbered menu, do either of the following:

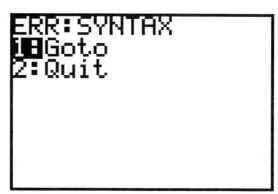

Figure 4.3

  a. press the number to the left of the choice you want—this is the fastest way—or

  b. position the cursor next to your choice and press ⎣ENTER⎦.

To return to the Home screen (Remember, "Quit to go Home."), press

[2:Quit].

The screen should look like Fig. 4.4, with a flashing cursor below the 7.

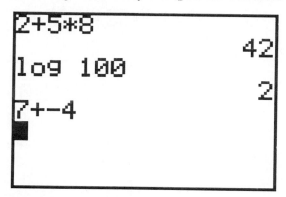

Figure 4.4

To return to the ERROR MESSAGE menu (see Fig. 4.3), press

ENTER .

Selecting [1:Goto] at this point causes the cursor to "go to" the source of the error and clears the Home screen of all data except the expression that contains the error. Generally, the Goto option will help you find your error.

1. If you have not already done so, press [1:Goto] now.
The cursor should flash on the subtraction symbol.

2. Press (-) to overwrite the subtraction symbol with a negative sign.

3. Press ENTER to re-execute the calculation.
You should obtain the expected result: 3.

4.2.4 Editing Expressions

Using Last Entry. When you press ENTER on the Home screen to evaluate an expression or execute an instruction, the expression or instruction is stored with other previous entries in a storage area called the Last Entry Stack. You can recall a prior entry from the Last Entry Stack, edit it, and then execute the edited instruction, as the following example illustrates.

Example 1   Doubling an Investment's Value

Problem You deposit $500 in a savings account earning 4.75% annual percentage rate (APR), compounded monthly. How long will it take for your investment to double in value?

Solution Because $4.75 \approx 5$ and $100 \div 5 = 20$, you might make an initial guess of 20 yr. To check the guess, do the following:

1. Press 2nd QUIT to return to the Home screen, if necessary.

2. Press CLEAR once or twice.
   On a line with text on the Home screen, CLEAR clears the text from the line.
   On a blank line on the Home screen, CLEAR clears the text from the entire screen.

3. Press

   500 [( ] **1** [+] **0** [.] **0475** [÷] **12** [ )] [^] [( ] **12** [×] **20** [ )] [ENTER] .

   (See Fig. 4.5.)

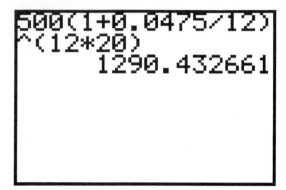

Figure 4.5

4. To display the results in a format more appropriate for calculations involving money,
   a. press

   [MODE]

   to display the Mode screen.
   b. Press [▼] [▶] [▶] [▶] to position the cursor over the 2.
   c. Press [ENTER] .
   The numerical display format is changed to two fixed decimal places (see Fig. 4.6).

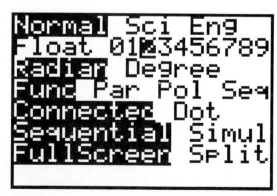

Figure 4.6

5. Press [2nd] [QUIT] to return to the Home screen.
6. Press [ENTER] to display the result in the new, two-decimal-place format (see Fig. 4.7).

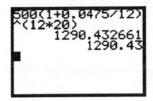

Figure 4.7

Our next guess should be quite a bit less than 20 yr, say 14 yr. In this case, do the following:

1. To edit the old expression, press

2. Evaluate the edited version by pressing

ENTER .

(See Fig. 4.8.)

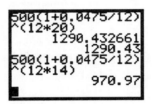

Figure 4.8

3. To change the number of years to 14.5, press

2nd ENTRY ◄ . 5 ENTER .

Notice that the final parenthesis can be left off and that all three results can be seen on the screen (see Fig. 4.9).

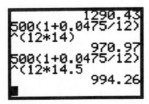

Figure 4.9

Continue this guess-and-check procedure until you obtain the accuracy you desire. Press 2nd ENTRY several times to observe how the Last Entry Stack has stored several prior entries.

Using the Edit Keys.   The Edit keys help you make effective use of your calculator (see Table 4.1).

TABLE 4.1

Key	Comments
◄ or ►	Moves the cursor within a line. These keys repeat.
▲ or ▼	Moves the cursor between the lines. These keys repeat.
2nd ◄	Moves the cursor to the beginning of expression. Can be used for fast-tracing on the Graph screen.
2nd ►	Moves the cursor to the end of the expression. Can be used for fast-tracing on the Graph screen.
ENTER	Evaluates an expression or executes an instruction. This key acts as a Pause key when graphing, press it a second time to resume graphing.
CLEAR	• On a line with text on the Home screen, this key clears (blanks) the current command line. • On a blank line on the Home screen, it clears the screen. • In an editor, it clears (blanks) the expression or value on which the cursor is located. It does not store zero as the value.
DEL	Deletes the character at the cursor. This key repeats.
2nd INS	Inserts characters at the underline cursor. To end insertion, press 2nd INS or a cursor-movement key.
2nd	Means the next key pressed is a 2nd operation (the blue operation to the left above a key). The cursor changes to an ↑. To cancel 2nd, press 2nd again.
ALPHA	Means the next key pressed is an ALPHA character (the gray character to the right above a key). The cursor changes to an A. To cancel ALPHA, press ALPHA or a cursor-movement key.
2nd A-LOCK	Sets ALPHA-LOCK. Each subsequent key press is an ALPHA character. The cursor changes to an A. To cancel ALPHA-LOCK, press ALPHA. Note that prompts for names automatically set the keyboard in ALPHA-LOCK.
X, T, θ	Allows you to enter an x in Function (Func) mode, a t in Parametric (Par) mode, or a θ in Polar (Pol) mode without pressing ALPHA first.

Display Cursors.   Four types of cursors indicate what will happen when you press the next key (see Table 4.2).

TABLE 4.2

Entry cursor	Solid blinking rectangle	The next keystroke is entered at the cursor; it overwrites any character.
INS (insert) cursor	Blinking underline	The next keystroke is inserted in front of the cursor location.
2nd cursor	Blinking ↑	The next keystroke is a 2nd operation.
ALPHA cursor	Blinking A	The next keystroke is an alphabetic character.

4.2.5   Scientific Notation and the Answer Key

The next example illustrates a geometric progression—a sequence of numbers that grows by a constant factor—while demonstrating some important features of your calculator.

Example 2   Generating a Geometric Sequence

Problem   Generate the terms in a geometric sequence that begins with 1.7×10^3 and grows by a constant factor of 100.

Solution   The method illustrates scientific notation entry and the LAST ANSWER (Ans) feature. To generate the sequence, do the following:

1. Return your calculator to Floating Point Numerical Display (Float) mode by pressing MODE ▼ ENTER .

2. Press 2nd QUIT to return to the Home screen.

3. Clear the Home screen by pressing CLEAR CLEAR .

4. To enter 1.7×10^3 onto the Home screen, press

    1 . **7** 2nd EE **3** ENTER .

Notice that entering the number in scientific notation did not cause the result to be displayed in scientific notation (see Fig. 4.10).

5. Press × **100**.

As soon as you press × *'Ans* * *' is displayed on the screen. **Ans** is a variable that contains the last calculated result, (see Fig. 4.11).*

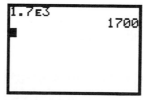

Figure 4.10

Figure 4.11

6. Press ENTER four times.

Each time you press ENTER *, the previous answer is multiplied by 100 and Ans is continually updated. Notice the display automatically becomes scientific notation when the number is too large (or too small) to display otherwise (see Fig. 4.12).*

7. Press ENTER twice to see the geometric progression continue.
Multiplication by 100 increases the exponent of ten by 2 each time (see Fig. 4.13).

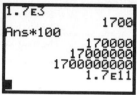

Figure 4.12

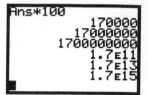

Figure 4.13

4.2.6   Working with Other Numerical Computation Features and Menus

Clear the Home screen and then try the following calculations.

1. **Integer arithmetic**

    To calculate -2 − -3 + -4 × 5, press

     (-) 2 − (-) 3 + (-) 4 × 5 ENTER .

2. **Rational-number arithmetic**

    To add the fractions $\frac{1}{3}$ and $\frac{4}{7}$, press

    1 ÷ 3 + 4 ÷ 7 MATH [1:Frac] ENTER .

3. **Real-number arithmetic**

    To approximate the principal square root of 10, press

    2nd √ 10 ENTER .

(See Fig. 4.14.)

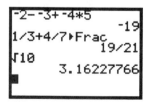

Figure 4.14

4. **Order of operations**

    To show that exponents take precedence over negation, and thus $(-6)^4 \neq -6^4$, press

    CLEAR ((-) 6) ^ 4 ENTER .

Then press

    (-) 6 ^ 4 ENTER .

and compare the results (see Fig. 4.15).

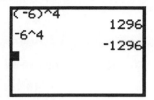

Figure 4.15

5. **Trig and angle computation**
To calculate tan 60° without switching to Degree mode, press

CLEAR TAN **60** 2nd ANGLE [1:°] ENTER .

Then press

2nd √ **3** ENTER .

and compare the results (see Fig. 4.16).

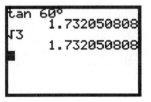

Figure 4.16

6. **Roots**
To evaluate $\sqrt[5]{-16807}$, press either

CLEAR **5** MATH [5:$^x\sqrt{\ }$] (−) **16807** ENTER

or

((−) **16807**) ^ (**1** ÷ **5**) ENTER .

(See Fig. 4.17).

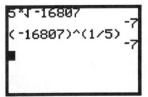

Figure 4.17

7. **Greatest integer function**
To determine the greatest integer less than or equal to -4.916, press

$\boxed{\text{MATH}}$ $\boxed{\blacktriangleright}$ [4:int] $\boxed{\text{(-)}}$ **4** $\boxed{\text{.}}$ **916** $\boxed{\text{ENTER}}$.

8. **Factorial**
To evaluate $10! = 10 \cdot 9 \cdot 8 \cdot 7 \cdot 6 \cdot 5 \cdot 4 \cdot 3 \cdot 2 \cdot 1$, press

10 $\boxed{\text{MATH}}$ $\boxed{\blacktriangleleft}$ [4:!] $\boxed{\text{ENTER}}$.

(See Fig. 4.18.)

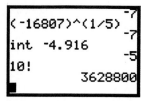

Figure 4.18

4.2.7   Computing with Lists

Next, set the display format to five fixed-decimal places as follows:

1. Press $\boxed{\text{MODE}}$.
2. Press $\boxed{\blacktriangledown}$ and then $\boxed{\blacktriangleright}$ six times.
3. Press $\boxed{\text{ENTER}}$.
4. Return to the Home screen by pressing $\boxed{\text{2nd}}$ $\boxed{\text{QUIT}}$.
5. Clear the Home Screen by pressing $\boxed{\text{CLEAR}}$.

1. To enter $\log (2^1)$, press

$\boxed{\text{LOG}}$ $\boxed{\text{(}}$ **2** $\boxed{\text{^}}$ **1** $\boxed{\text{)}}$ $\boxed{\text{ENTER}}$.

2. To enter $\log (2^2)$, press

$\boxed{\text{2nd}}$ $\boxed{\text{ENTRY}}$ $\boxed{\blacktriangleleft}$ $\boxed{\blacktriangleleft}$ **2** $\boxed{\text{ENTER}}$.

3. To enter $\log (2^3)$, press

$\boxed{\text{2nd}}$ $\boxed{\text{ENTRY}}$ $\boxed{\blacktriangleleft}$ $\boxed{\blacktriangleleft}$ **3** $\boxed{\text{ENTER}}$.

(See Fig. 4.19.)

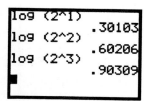

Figure 4.19

Do you see the pattern? A rule of logarithms states that for positive numbers x, $\log(x^n) = n\log(x)$. To see the pattern in a different way,

1. press

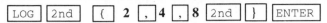

2. press and hold ▶ to see the third item in the "list."
(See Fig. 4.20.)

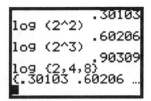

Figure 4.20

The curly braces { } are used to enclose an ordered set of numbers. Although set notation is used, the TI-82 treats {2, 4, 8} as a **list**, an ordered set of numbers on which it can operate. You can add, subtract, multiply, and divide lists, but you operate on sets differently, using operations such as union and intersection. So lists and sets are mathematically different and have different operations. The *TI-82 Guidebook* has a chapter on lists. You also can learn about lists through experimentation; try using them in various ways and observe the results.

4.2.8 Using Variables

Example 3   Finding the Height of a Triangle

Problem A triangle encloses an area of 75 cm^2 and has a base of 11 cm. What is its height?

Solution Recall that the area is given by one half the base times the height: $A = (1/2)bh$. Therefore to find the height, do the following:

1. To put your calculator in Floating Point mode,
   a. press MODE and
   b. select the Float option.
2. Return to and clear the Home screen.
3. To store the value 11 as the variable B, press

11 STO▶ ALPHA B ENTER .

4. Because one half the base is about 5, the height should be about 15. Therefore press

15 STO▶ ALPHA H 2nd : (1 ÷ 2) 2nd A-LOCK B H ENTER .

(See Fig. 4.21.)

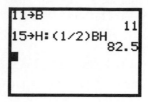

Figure 4.21

5. Our guess was too big, so enter

$\boxed{\text{2nd}}$ $\boxed{\text{ENTRY}}$ $\boxed{\blacktriangle}$ 14 $\boxed{\text{ENTER}}$.

(See Fig. 4.22.)

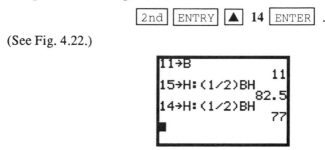

Figure 4.22

The next guess would be between 13 and 14 and would require inserting extra digits in front of $\boxed{\text{STO} \blacktriangleright}$ (press $\boxed{\text{2nd}}$ $\boxed{\text{INS}}$ at the appropriate location). Continue the guess-and-check process to practice using the editing features of your calculator and to find the height with an error of no more than 0.01.

4.3 _____ Function Graphing and Table Building

Graphing and table building on the TI-82 involve the top row of keys. There are four graphing modes on the TI-82: Function, Parametric, Polar, and Sequence. Each has a corresponding table-building mode. Thus changing the setting on the fourth line of the Mode screen affects both graphing and table building (see Fig. 4.23).

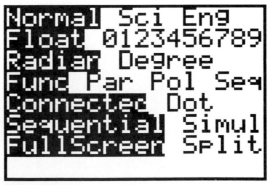

Figure 4.23

For this section, be sure your calculator is in Function mode (Func). In Section 4.4 we explore the Parametric and Polar modes. The remainder of this section is built around various methods for solving equations on the TI-82, using the example

$$\cos x = \tan x \text{ for } 0 \le x \le 1.$$

4.3.1   Method A: Graphing Each Side and Zooming In

1. Enter each side of the equation as a function on the Y= screen by pressing

   $\boxed{\text{Y=}}$ $\boxed{\text{COS}}$ $\boxed{\text{X,T,θ}}$ $\boxed{\text{ENTER}}$ $\boxed{\text{TAN}}$ $\boxed{\text{X,T,θ}}$ $\boxed{\text{ENTER}}$.

   (See Fig. 4.24.)

Figure 4.24

2. Press $\boxed{\text{ZOOM}}$ [4:ZDecimal].
   Watch as the curves are graphed in sequence. The vertical lines are pseudo-asymptotes of y = tan x. The calculator is actually connecting points that are off the screen (see Fig. 4.25).

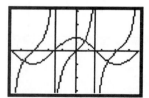

Figure 4.25

3. Press $\boxed{\text{WINDOW}}$ to see what portion of the plane is being used for graphing. The viewing rectangle, or window, being used is [xMin, xMax] by [yMin, yMax], in this case [-4.7, 4.7] by [-3.1, 3.1]. Because xscl =1 and yscl = 1, the tick marks on each axis are one unit apart (see Fig. 4.26).

Figure 4.26

4. Press $\boxed{\text{TRACE}}$.

Observe the coordinate readout at the bottom of the screen as you press and release $\boxed{\blacktriangleright}$ repeatedly. Stop when $x = 0.7$. The graphs appear to intersect at $x = 0.7$; actually this is a rough approximation of the solution we seek for $\cos x = \tan x$ for $0 \leq x \leq 1$ (see Fig. 4.27).

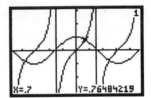

Figure 4.27

Now you can probably see why the fourth ZOOM feature is called Zoom Decimal (ZDecimal). It adjusted the viewing window to give a nice *decimal* readout. Notice the 1 in the upper right-hand corner of the screen. It lets you know that you are tracing on Y_1, which in this case is $\cos x$.

5. Press $\boxed{\blacktriangledown}$ to move the Trace cursor to Y_2.

The x-value does not change, but the y-value does, because you are now tracing on $Y_2 = \tan x$. Notice the 2 in the upper right-hand corner of the screen (see Fig. 4.28).

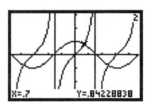

Figure 4.28

6. Press $\boxed{\text{GRAPH}}$.

The Trace cursor, the coordinate readout, and the number in the upper right-hand corner of the screen all disappear and only the graph itself is displayed (see Fig. 4.29).

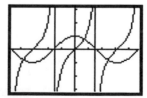

Figure 4.29

7. Press any of the cursor-movement keys. You now are using a free-moving cursor that is not confined to either of the graphs. Notice that this cursor looks different from the Trace cursor.

8. Experiment with all four cursor-movement keys.

Watch the screen coordinate readout change. Move to the point (0.7, 0.8). Notice $y = 0.8$ is not the value of either function at $x = 0.7$, it is just the y-coordinate of a dot (pixel) on the graphing screen (see Fig. 4.30). Notice that the free-moving cursor yields a nice decimal readout for both x and y. This is because we used Zoom Decimal to set the viewing window.

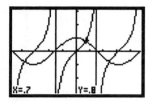

Figure 4.30

Using ZOOM Box. This option lets you use the cursor to select opposite corners of a "box" to define a new viewing window. Continuing the example from above, do the following:

1. To return to the Graph screen with the cursor at (0, 0), and to select the Zoom Box option, press $\boxed{\text{Y=}}$ and then $\boxed{\text{ZOOM}}$ [1:BOX].
    (See Fig. 4.31.)

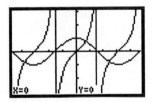

Figure 4.31

2. To select a new viewing window of [0, 1] by [0, 1.2], which will limit x so that $0 \le x \le 1$,
    a. press $\boxed{\text{ENTER}}$ to select the point $(0, 0)$ as one corner of the new viewing window and
    b. use the cursor-movement keys to move to the opposite corner $(1, 1.2)$ (see Fig. 4.32).

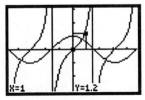

Figure 4.32

3. To select (1, 1.2) as the opposite corner of the new viewing window, press

ENTER .

The graphs of the two functions will be drawn in the new viewing window (see Fig. 4.33).

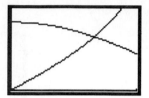

Figure 4.33

4. To remove the cursor and coordinates from the screen, press

GRAPH .

5. To verify that the new viewing window is [0, 1] by [0, 1.2], press

WINDOW .

Notice that xscl and yscl are still both equal to one. The Zoom Box option does change the scale settings (see Fig. 4.34).

6. To approximate the solution as $x \approx 0.6702$,

    a. press TRACE and

    b. use the cursor-movement keys to move to the point of intersection (see Fig. 4.35).

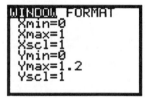

Figure 4.34

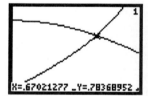

Figure 4.35

Finding an error bound. Next, using the approximate solution we found in number 6 above, we want to find the error bound for *x*, as follows:

1. To return to and clear the Home screen, press

2nd QUIT CLEAR .

2. To see the approximate solution, press

X,T,θ ENTER .

3. Press

VARS [1:Window] [7:Δx] ENTER .

The value of Δx is the horizontal distance between consecutive pixels in the current viewing window, which in this case is about 0.011. This is an error bound for x. Our approximate solution, 0.6702, has an error of at most 0.011.

We need to pick *x*Min and *x*Max so that they are closer together to decrease this error bound (see Fig. 4.36).

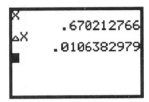

Figure 4.36

Do the following:

1. To enter the smaller window of [0.5, 0.8] by [0.6, 1.0], press

(See Fig. 4.37.)

2. To move to the point of intersection—approximately (0.666, 0.786), press

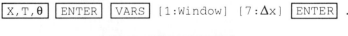

and then after the graph is drawn use the cursor-movement keys (see Fig. 4.38).

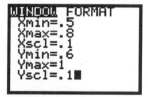

Figure 4.37

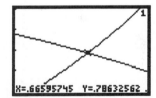

Figure 4.38

3. To display the previous approximation and error bound along with the new and improved approximation and error bound (see Fig. 4.39), press

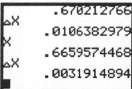

Figure 4.39

4. Press

$$\boxed{\text{COS}} \quad \boxed{\text{X,T,}\theta} \quad \boxed{\text{ENTER}} \quad \boxed{\text{TAN}} \quad \boxed{\text{X,T,}\theta} \quad \boxed{\text{ENTER}} \; .$$

From this, you should see that cos x and tan x are nearly, but not exactly, equal when $x = 0.6659...$ (see Fig. 4.40).

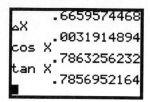

Figure 4.40

4.3.2   Method B: Table Building

The Y= screen is used to enter functions for both graphing and table building. To build a table, do as follows:

1. Press $\boxed{\text{Y=}}$ to check that $Y_1 = \cos x$ and $Y_2 = \tan x$ (see Fig. 4.41).

Figure 4.41

2. To reveal the Table Setup screen, press

$$\boxed{\text{2nd}} \quad \boxed{\text{TblSet}} \; .$$

3. Press

$$\mathbf{0} \; \boxed{\text{ENTER}} \; \mathbf{0} \; \boxed{.} \; \mathbf{1} \; \boxed{\text{ENTER}}$$

and ensure the Auto option is selected for both the independent variable (x) and the dependent variable (y) (see Fig. 4.42).

Figure 4.42

4. Press

$$\boxed{\text{2nd}} \quad \boxed{\text{TABLE}}$$

and notice that the first x-value is the TblMin (= 0) and that the increment from one row to the next in the x column is Δ Tbl (= 0.1) (see Fig. 4.43).

5. Press $\boxed{\blacktriangledown}$ repeatedly to move down the x column of the table to $X = 0.7$. Notice that the solution lies between $x = 0.6$ and $x = 0.7$ (see Fig. 4.44).

Figure 4.43

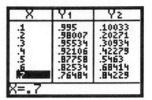

Figure 4.44

Use the cursor-movement keys to move around the table and explore. Pay attention to the readout at the bottom of the screen as you move to different "cells" in the table.

6. Press

$\boxed{\text{2nd}}$ $\boxed{\text{TblSet}}$ **0** $\boxed{.}$ **6** $\boxed{\text{ENTER}}$ **0** $\boxed{.}$ **01** $\boxed{\text{ENTER}}$.

The value of Δ Tbl will serve as the error bound for table building, just as Δx did for graphing (see Fig. 4.45).

7. Press $\boxed{\text{2nd}}$ $\boxed{\text{TABLE}}$ and then press $\boxed{\blacktriangledown}$ repeatedly until you reach $x = 0.67$. This is a solution with an error of at most 0.01 (see Fig. 4.46).

Figure 4.45

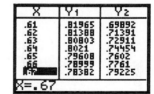

Figure 4.46

4.3.3   Method C: Solving an Equivalent Equation

To solve $\cos x = \tan x$ for $0 \le x \le 1$, you can solve the equivalent equation $\cos x - \tan x = 0$ for the same interval. To do this, follow these steps:

1. Press

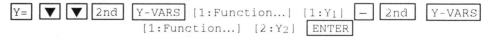

$\boxed{\text{Y=}}$ $\boxed{\blacktriangledown}$ $\boxed{\blacktriangledown}$ $\boxed{\text{2nd}}$ $\boxed{\text{Y-VARS}}$ [1:Function...] [1:Y_1] $\boxed{-}$ $\boxed{\text{2nd}}$ $\boxed{\text{Y-VARS}}$ [1:Function...] [2:Y_2] $\boxed{\text{ENTER}}$

(See Fig. 4.47 on page 62).

2. To deselect Y_1 and Y_2, press

$$\boxed{\blacktriangle}\ \boxed{\blacktriangle}\ \boxed{\blacktriangleleft}\ \boxed{\text{ENTER}}\ \boxed{\blacktriangle}\ \boxed{\text{ENTER}}.$$

Now only Y_3 should have its equals sign highlighted (see Fig. 4.48).

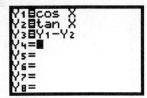

Figure 4.47

Figure 4.48

3. To see the graph of $y = \cos x - \tan x$ in a "friendly" viewing window, press

$\boxed{\text{ZOOM}}$ [4:ZDecimal]; and after the graph is drawn, press $\boxed{\text{TRACE}}\ \boxed{\text{2nd}}\ \boxed{\blacktriangleright}\ \boxed{\blacktriangleright}\ \boxed{\blacktriangleright}$.

Notice $\boxed{\text{2nd}}\ \boxed{\blacktriangleright}$ moves the cursor five pixels to the right for fast tracing (see Fig. 4.49).

4. To enter the Zoom Factors screen, press

$\boxed{\text{ZOOM}}\ \boxed{\blacktriangleright}$ [4:SetFactors...]

and enter 10 as both the horizontal and the vertical magnification factor by pressing

10 $\boxed{\text{ENTER}}$ **10** $\boxed{\text{ENTER}}$.

(See Fig. 4.50.)

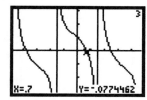

Figure 4.49

Figure 4.50

5. To center your zoom-in at the point $(x, y) = (0.7, 0)$, press

$\boxed{\text{ZOOM}}$ [2:ZoomIn] $\boxed{\text{2nd}}\ \boxed{\blacktriangleright}\ \boxed{\blacktriangleright}\ \boxed{\blacktriangleright}$

(see Fig. 4.51) and press $\boxed{\text{ENTER}}$ to zoom in.

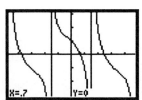

Figure 4.51

6. After the graph is redrawn, you can obtain the same approximation that was found by Method B by pressing

$$\boxed{\text{TRACE}}\ \boxed{\blacktriangleleft}\ \boxed{\blacktriangleleft}\ \boxed{\blacktriangleleft}\ .$$

Check the value of Δx; it is the same as the ΔTbl in Method B! (See Fig. 4.52).

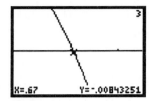

Figure 4.52

4.3.4   Other Equation-solving Methods

Traditional algebra and trigonometry can be used to determine the exact solution is

$$x = \sin^{-1} \frac{-1 + \sqrt{5}}{2}$$

Do the following:

1. To evaluate this expression on your calculator, press

$$\boxed{\text{2nd}}\ \boxed{\text{SIN}^{-1}}\ \boxed{(}\ \boxed{(}\ \boxed{(-)}\ \mathbf{1}\ \boxed{+}\ \boxed{\text{2nd}}\ \boxed{\sqrt{\ }}\ \mathbf{5}\ \boxed{)}\ \boxed{\div}\ \mathbf{2}\ \boxed{)}\ \boxed{\text{ENTER}}\ .$$

You obtain an approximation that is accurate to 10 decimal places. It should be consistent with those found by Methods A, B, and C, and it is (see Fig. 4.53).

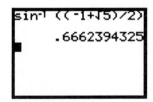

Figure 4.53

2. Set up your Y= screen as you did for Method C. Then, to obtain a graph, press

$$\boxed{\text{ZOOM}}\ [\text{4:ZDecimal}].$$

3. Press $\boxed{\text{2nd}}\ \boxed{\text{CALC}}\ [\text{2:root}].$
This should result in a prompt requesting a Lower Bound (see Fig. 4.54).

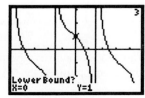

Figure 4.54

4. Because we are seeking a solution for $0 \le x \le 1$, the lower bound should be $x = 0$; so press

$\boxed{\text{ENTER}}$.

5. To move the cursor to $x = 1$, press

$\boxed{\text{2nd}}$ $\boxed{\blacktriangleright}$ $\boxed{\text{2nd}}$ $\boxed{\blacktriangleright}$

followed by $\boxed{\text{ENTER}}$ to enter it as the upper bound.

6. Move the Trace cursor to $x = 0.7$ and enter it as your guess by pressing

$\boxed{\blacktriangleleft}$ $\boxed{\blacktriangleleft}$ $\boxed{\blacktriangleleft}$ $\boxed{\text{ENTER}}$.

The calculator should yield a root value of $x = 0.66623943$ (see Fig. 4.55).

7. To compare the value found using the root finding and the value found in Part 1 above, press

$\boxed{\text{X,T,}\theta}$ $\boxed{\text{ENTER}}$.

They match perfectly to 10 decimal places! (See Fig. 4.56.)

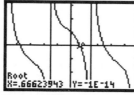

Figure 4.55

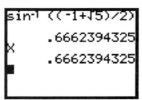

Figure 4.56

8. To use the Solve option to solve the equation, press

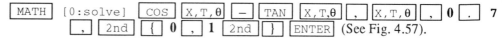

$\boxed{\text{MATH}}$ [0:solve] $\boxed{\text{COS}}$ $\boxed{\text{X,T,}\theta}$ $\boxed{-}$ $\boxed{\text{TAN}}$ $\boxed{\text{X,T,}\theta}$ $\boxed{,}$ $\boxed{\text{X,T,}\theta}$ $\boxed{,}$ $\boxed{0}$ $\boxed{.}$ 7 $\boxed{,}$ $\boxed{\text{2nd}}$ $\boxed{\{}$ $\boxed{0}$ $\boxed{,}$ 1 $\boxed{\text{2nd}}$ $\boxed{\}}$ $\boxed{\text{ENTER}}$ (See Fig. 4.57).

Notice the order of the information you entered:

a. the expression that is set equal to zero,

b. the variable being solved for,

c. a guess at the solution, and

d. a list of the lower and upper bounds.

Figure 4.57

There are many other ways to solve equations on the TI-82. One that should be mentioned is using the Intersect option on the CALCULATE menu in conjunction with Method A. Set up your Y= screen as in Method A and try it. As you learn more mathematics and more about your calculator, you will discover more ways to solve equations.

4.4 _____ Other Graphing and Table Building

4.4.1 Parametric Graphing and Table Building

Parametric equations are ideal tools for representing and solving problems in geometry and the physics of motion. The TI-82 has a built-in parametric graphing utility. This utility is similar to the function graphing utility and is almost as easy to use. To graph a parametric curve, you

- select the Parametric (Par) mode on the Mode screen,
- type the desired equations in the Y= screen,
- set the intervals for t, x, and y using the Window screen, and
- press $\boxed{\text{GRAPH}}$.

Parametric equations are written in the form

$$x = f(t) \quad \text{and} \quad y = g(t).$$

In this setting, t is called a parameter; however, t actually is an independent variable, not a parameter in the sense that m and b are parameters in the equation $y = mx + b$. Unlike the independent variable x we are used to in Function-graphing mode, the parameter t is not a plotted, visible coordinate; it is hidden from view when we look at a parametric curve. When we use the TRACE feature, we see a readout of the parameter t and the coordinates x and y, which are the dependent variables of the parametric representation.

Example 4   Graphing the Curve Represented by Parametric Equations

Problem Graph the curve represented by the following parametric equations:

$$x = t^2 \quad \text{and} \quad y = t - 1 \quad \text{for} \ -2 \leq t \leq 2.$$

Solution To solve this problem, follow these steps:

1. Press $\boxed{\text{MODE}}$ to enter the Mode screen and
   a. select Parametric Graphing (Par) and
   b. choose the default (leftmost) settings for the other mode settings.
2. Because we are in Parametric mode, pressing $\boxed{\text{X,T,}\theta}$ will yield the letter t. To enter the given parametric equations, press

$$\boxed{\text{Y=}} \quad \boxed{\text{X,T,}\theta} \quad \boxed{x^2} \quad \boxed{\text{ENTER}} \quad \boxed{\text{X,T,}\theta} \quad \boxed{-} \quad \mathbf{1} \quad \boxed{\text{ENTER}} .$$

The screen should look like Fig. 4.58.

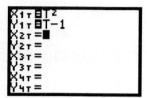

Figure 4.58

3. Press ⌷WINDOW⌷ and then set the Window screen as shown in Fig. 4.59. (Note that you won't be able to see the entire screen at once because it has too many lines.)

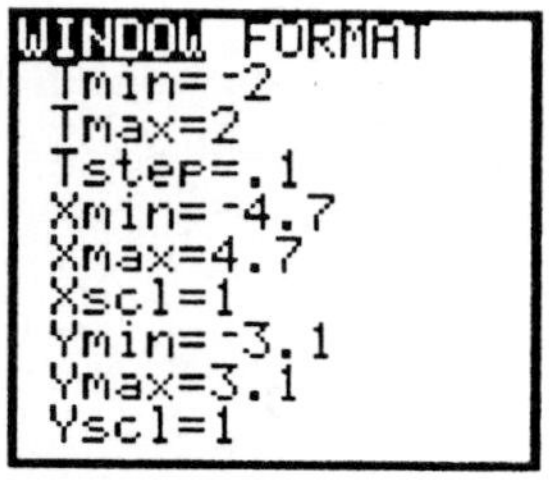

Figure 4.59

The *t*step on the Parametric Window screen is the change between the successive *t*-values that the calculator uses to compute and plot (x, y) pairs. In this case, the *t*step of 0.1 will yield 40 steps from the *t*Min of -2 to the *t*Max of 2. Thus 41 points will be calculated and plotted, with the points corresponding to

$$t = -2.0, -1.9, -1.8, -1.7, \ldots, 1.9, 2.0.$$

Table 4.3 shows the numerical relationship between the parameter *t* and the coordinates *x* and *y* for some of the points to be plotted.

The last two columns of Table 4.3 determine the (x, y) coordinate pairs to be plotted. The values of the parameter *t* will not appear on the graph.

You can create a table like Table 4.3 on your calculator as follows:

1. Press

[2nd] [TblSet] [(-)] **2** [ENTER] **0** [.] **1** [ENTER].

(See Fig. 4.60.)

TABLE 4.3

t	$x = t^2$	$y = t - 1$
-2.0	4.00	-3.0
-1.9	3.61	-2.9
-1.8	3.24	-2.8
-1.7	2.89	-2.7
.	.	.
.	.	.
.	.	.
1.9	3.61	0.9
2.0	4.00	1.0

Figure 4.60

2. Then press

[2nd] [TABLE]

(See Figure 4.61).

3. Press [GRAPH] to yield the plot shown in Fig. 4.62.
Because we are in Connected mode, the plotted points in Fig. 4.62 are connected by line segments.

To see only the 41 plotted points,

1. choose the Dot mode from the Mode screen and

2. press [GRAPH] again.

(See Fig. 4.63.)

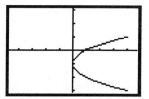

Figure 4.61

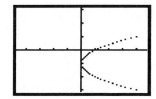

Figure 4.62

Figure 4.63

Return to Connected mode and use the TRACE feature and the left and right cursor-movement keys to explore the graph numerically. Notice that the values of the parameter *t* and the *x*- and *y*-coordinates are all shown on the screen (see Fig. 4.64 (a) and (b)). Can you find the six points that correspond to the completed rows of the table shown in Figure 4.61?

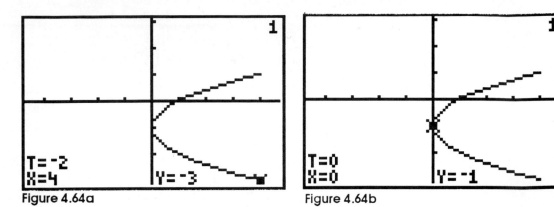

Figure 4.64a   Figure 4.64b

4.4.2   Polar Equation Graphing

The Polar Equation graphing mode is similar to the other graphing modes.

Example 5   Graphing Two Equations Simultaneously

Problem Graph $r = 9\sin 5\theta$ and $r = 9$.
Solution

1. Press [MODE] (see Fig. 4.65) and

Figure 4.65

a. select Polar (Pol) mode and Simultaneous (Simul) mode and

b. choose the defaults for the other modes.

2. Press [Y=] to display the Polar Equation screen.

3. To define the two desired equations, press

9 [SIN] 5 [X,T,θ] [ENTER] 9 [ENTER] .

(See Fig. 4.66.)

Figure 4.66

4. Press ZOOM [6:ZStandard].

The graph of r = 9 is supposed to be a circle of radius 9 centered at the pole. The circle circumscribes the five-petaled rose curve r = 9sin5θ (see Fig. 4.67).

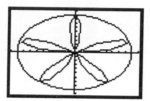

Figure 4.67

5. To set θMax = π, press

WINDOW ▼ ▼ 2nd π ENTER .

6. To "square up" the window, press

ZOOM [5:ZSquare] .

The entire rose curve is plotted using the interval 0 ≤ θ ≤ π. Press TRACE *and explore the two curves (see Fig. 4.68).*

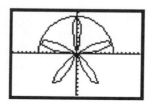

Figure 4.68